THE MUSINGS of SHMU'AL YAHU

Published by:
Lulu.com

ISBN 978-1-6671-2716-3

Printed in the United States of America

This book is dedicated to you...

Life can get the best of you anytime and it can happen to anyone. No one is except from this experience. Some people lose focus which causes them to get to this point. In the valley deep which seems to feel like no way out, when it feels like your back is up against the wall and you feel like you have no one in your corner; someone is always there. It's at the lowest point in your life when the enemy would like to separate you from all that you love to cause you to lose your soul. What are you going to do? Who do you run to?

Attitude of how you approach a situation will determine the outcome. The wrong attitude will leave you in despair, feeling hopeless, believing the absolute worse and cause you to drown in self-pity. The right attitude will have you looking at the situation in a new light. Full of joy, hope, and causing self reflection on ones character and the things that need to change in order for you to do better. ATTITUDE IS EVERYTHING!

You are not always right. Failing to see things in another perspective clouds your vision and also distorts it. The full spectrum cannot be seen if you're not willing to view it in another way. A lot of times we cause our own woes to come upon us because of bad choices and decisions. Those choices and decisions can lead you down a road you weren't intending to go but because of unchecked issues one day it will all come to a head and then **BOOM, EXPLOSION.**

What to do, what to do? What do you do in this moment? Do you continue the course until the end causes you to lose your life or do you make a radical change to live the life that you've always envisioned. Some people chose the same course and lose their life while others chose the latter and make a change. Why would someone chose not to change and continue the same discourse? **HOPE!** Some people have no hope. Where there is no hope there is no life. Try living life with no hope, it's difficult and hard. Running on fumes of emptiness will not get you far only lose and left behind. When despair takes over the enemy will leave seeds of delusions speaking words of hopelessness that will dig you deeper and deeper into depression because of the belief of the enemy lies. When you start to believe the lies of the enemy roots begin to take place and who you were begins to vanish and becomes non-existent. Without hope there is no life. Without life there is only death and with death being the end game there is nothing else. Then the question gets asked, what can help to keep and maintain hope?

Hope cannot be found in material things because those things will lose value and become worthless. Hope cannot be found in another person because people come and people go. Hope cannot be found in riches because riches can be lost in an instant. Hope can only be found in YAHUAH. He is your shield and buckler, your strong tower, your present help in a time of need. It's when we take situations into our own hands that we lose hope and focus. He should be our lead and our head for without HIM there is no guidance. Those who are called will hear because everybody doesn't belong to him. He chasten those whom he loves. No chasten is good, it's only to get you back in line. Those that endure chasten their souls shall be saved but those that resist it will die in their sin like a wayward son. Take chasten as a joy and rejoice that the FATHER loves you with an everlasting love and that you belong to him. For many are called but few chose. The chasten of your soul brings you to a place of repentance, a place of contemplation and a place of realization. Some accept it while others reject it. Those that accept it claim victory in their life over all those things that brought them to that low estate. Those that reject it are crushed and left to drown in their own sin.

AS A MAN THINKETH SO IS HE. What do you think about yourself? How do you view yourself? What has shapes the views about yourself?

Rock Bottom is a place that can compel someone to change or they will remain the same and utterly it will lead to their dismiss.

Will it make you or break you, that's the question. People have a perception about life saying if you've had the same opportunities as everyone else but people views can be distorted because everyone doesn't have the same mindset. Everyone's mindset isn't as strong as others may be. Judge all you want without walking in a man's shoes and you will always be a fool. Three individuals can grow up in the same household learning the same values yet three different pathways are pursued in life. We all are own persons' with our own views and thoughts on things and the direction we take. The stigma the world places on people is foolishness. If you don't have this, if you haven't obtained that, if you're going through this or that, if you don't have a degree, if you don't have this car, if you don't have this house, if you haven't obtained a certain amount of success by a certain age what does your life really mean. What does the world know, NOTHING! All these things will pass away and at your life's end what will people remember you for? You can't take anything with you but your life will testify against you on the day of judgment and what does your life say about you? What do your thoughts say about you?

What is time to YAHUAH? Our life is but a mere vapor, breath of air, here one second and gone the next. So what is time; seconds, minutes, hours, days, months, years when you really examine what time is it passes as fast as you can think about it. Time is something you can't get back. It's something experienced for a moment and then it's gone. So, what do we do with time while we have it? Do you waste it or do you cherish it? Time is to be cherish but a lot of times we waste it. Wasted opportunities, wasted moments and a wasted life. Who dictates the life we lead and what do we do it for? What do we chase in this life that's important? The world passes by with the things that mean nothing, absolutely nothing! We give importance to this world that means nothing. What do we take with us when we leave this earth other than how we treated people. Were we harsh with our attitudes, rude with our words, did we treat other's one way and treated other people another way? Would we want people to treat us the way we treated everyone else. That is a great question. How do we view people? Do we think of ourselves more than what we actually are to feel good about ourselves? This is something to consider.

Lose those who mean you no good! Get rid of them out of your life. If they're not helping you then they're hurting you. People should challenge you to be a better version of yourself. Extracting the real you is tough and difficult. You have years of layers that have hidden who you really are. Who cares about what the world says about what's going on because in actuality they're living in a dream of false per-tense and hope. They believe in themselves and no one else. Their life is dictated by society and what society says is what you should be doing, who you should be and what direction you should be going in. What do they know; ABSOULTELY NOTHING! Forget the world and their concepts of things because it will leave you depressed and feeling worthless. Find yourself in the counsel of the Most High YAHUAH. In HIM we move and have our being. It's in HIM we find life and purpose not according to the world standards but according to HIS. You will lose family, friends and be considered an outcast. I would rather be an outcast for YAHUAH than to be apart of a world that's going to be destroyed. If the world means that much to you, you're not fit for the kingdom. Forsake the world and all their ways and live a life for YAHUAH. Your works will follow you and your life will testify against you. What will it say? Your thoughts, your deeds, your speech, and the secret things will speak against you and be a witness.

Repent, forgive, and seek the kingdom of YAHUAH. From my own reflection of life I found it all to be vanity. The things we believe we want is vanity. Only true joy can be found in YAHUAH. That's the only fulfilling thing in life along with helping people. Things mean nothing, relationships mean nothing, family means nothing, partying means nothing, money means nothing and your career means nothing. The only thing that means something is YAHUAH! So, remember when you get to your lowest point in life think upon the name of YAHUAH and he will sustain you and get you through.

THE WRITINGS

GET DOWN

Complicated schemes rob you of your dreams wanna be supreme by all and any means claim it for the team what does it really mean if in the end you whind up losing everything through the back alley ways finding time to play but along the way you end up losing your way fictitious alibis giving rhymes and reasons living through the seasons tensions building you wanna be pleasing ending in the seasons for the same reasons better off alone and by yourself because no one appreciates the help they love you the most when you're gone that's when they have a sad song realizing what they done wrong who wins in the end living life in sin death is what awaits your soul is at stake don't make the same mistakes to have your mama crying at your wake soul ceasing soul releasing not for street reasons let your life to YAHUAH be pleasing who cares who you lose on the way side your soul captivate it when facing trepidation this ain't a vacation this is the real fight you only got one life so you better live it right don't believe the deceiving devices they will kill you in end glitter ain't gold it falls off in the wind

Fasing it out troubling times tryna wrap your mind the enemy keep dropping dimes telling them lies you don't want to face the facts that some people just put on a act to serve they own purpose is it all worth it you hear the crickets chirping turn a blind eye and lose in the end you only got yourself to blame that's your claim to fame

What you wanna lose it might be your life now you think about it wasn't living it right you better wanna fight for your soul don't let the enemy take control don't let him stomp you out stand on your feet scream and shout give a praise to the Most High from the top of your lungs let him fill your heart with a new song over flowing waters something to drink on

Man shall not live by bread alone but by every word that proceeds out of the mouth of the most high YAHUAH put your life on line you'll save when it comes to the end of times otherwise hear depart I never knew you I'm just to hear to school I hope these lesson are getting interjected into your brain still tryna maintain from going insane but with YAHUAH spirit my mind is kept at peace feel the release and the tension cease kill that monstrous beast

We've Had Enough

Souls caught in the crossfire there's a need impeding doom the righteous won't concede down till the end witness the greed as the world all around continues to feed off the wickedness fill the cup the righteous seed has had enough grid up our loins we stepping up prepared for this war warriors we be tough sword in our hands ready to die no longer no more will we let this this wickedness fly free the captives trapped in their minds you don't wanna receive have a nice day as we continue to pave the way righteous judgement we ain't here to condemn just pass the word even if to some it may seem absurd die for our actions and that's the word we bout it been bout it no doubt about it YAHUAH we can't live without him

We've had enough you see deeply we grieve but we stand strong we've had enough

Dear to lose family and friends for YAH sake die for his truth understanding some don't have to this truth some don't grab hold self righteous that's what they say judge by my actions don't you get treated the right way when you don't agree it's perceived as being mean but someone like me you need on your team a true tried friend yes indeed love covers over a multitude of sins stop grieving the spirit it's time to truly win put off the old man let him die within and watch as your life become renewed again some ain't meant to get it just keep presenting the truth you don't know who YAH is saving don't be like Jonah refusing to speak the truth who are you to say who deserves this truth your life should show that YAH is real to be the burden of proof his word is the steel

We've had enough you see deeply we grieve but we stand strong we've had enough

Snakes and fakes will be revealed in the end contrary living be deeply infested with sin self check look at the man in the mirror if you're connected the picture will become clearer check yourself before you wreck yourself self righteousness is bad for your health the wars come to make you strong to expose you so you can correct the wrong the refining fire to burn and purge don't use the excuse of only being a man because YAHUAH through his son gave you the power masters of the universe sword in your hand the strength of the spirit if your ears are open then you can hear it calling for an uprising to stand for righteous sake it don't matter even if your life is at stake because what's to come can't be compared to the present

We've had enough you see deeply we grieve but we stand strong we've had enough

Brother

I don't have any animosity against my brother even if he's from another mother it's enough hate against us for me to hate my brother Yo word to the mother envying and jealousy we need to unite don't believe the hype cause they ain't gone save us no matter the fight unless we REPENT and return we'll continue to learn salvation is what we yearn

Brother brother we all that we got why stand on the block opp and get shoot brother we need to get rid of this hate before it's too late brother oh brother he's not your enemy why so much hate brother oh brother

We need the most high YAHUAH or we can't get by no matter how hard we try we'll all just die living a lie begging our oppressors trusting our enemies when we be the ones that they're envying because we're the Apple of his eye

But we still rather continue in the foot steps of our forefathers they seen YAHUAH work yet they chose to turn their backs because they didn't want to listen now us the children we're suffering because of false religion making those same decisions

Brother brother we all that we got why stand on the block opp and get shoot brother we need to get rid of this hate before it's too late brother oh brother he's not your enemy why so much hate brother oh brother

We need the most high YAHUAH or we can't get by no matter how hard we try we'll all just die living a lie begging our oppressors trusting our enemies when we be the ones that they're envying because we're the Apple of his eye oh brother

REPENT and return back to YAHUAH His laws status and commandments Believe in YAHUSHA our brother who sacrificed his life for you

YAHUAH is standing there with open arms why remain slaves to your sins when he's given the gift of life oh brother hear my cry

If a man say, I love YAH, and hates his brother, he is a liar: for he that loves not his brother whom he has seen, how can he love YAH whom he has not seen? YAHUCHANON RI'SHON (1 JOHN) 4:20 CEPHER

Come Bodly

I know sometimes in life it can get down right hard and difficult where we feel alone lost and broke but I know a source that can help us cope just call on his name and seek his ways then you'll see the end of your wandering days

Corrupted soul corrupted spirit does anyone dare come near it the cry the pull the longing sick and tired of listening whispering in the dark false delusions coming from the heart believing the lies of the enemy shame to call on his name believing that he cant understand the pain flipped collars scarf covering the face its cold on the outside but he offers a warm place the plight of the mind which does damage in the end because we remain convince that we can't be delivered from this sin the thing that supersede came from above and delivered us the fathers plan was to make everything right so that we might have a right to the tree of life the life we lead sometimes bleeds he just don't bandage he heals the wounds and supply's the need we just gotta believe

Come boldly unto the throne of grace so that we may obtain mercy for we have not a high priest which cannot be touched with the feelings of infirmities

For we have not a High Priest which cannot be touched with the feeling of our infirmities; but was in all points tempted like as we are, yet without sin. Let us therefore come boldly unto the throne of grace, that we may obtain mercy, and find grace to help in time of need. IVRIY (HEBREWS) 4:15-16 □□ CEPHER

We give your name all praise
Y A H U A H
We REPENT of our wicked ways
Please forgive our sin
So that we may live again
We give your name all praise

I Feel Some Type of Way

People really don't wanna let it go and it really does show because the life that they live just goes with the flow following the crowd everywhere that they go who will be the one to say people there is a better way a lonely road it's on some people you have to leave alone and you're running out of time so what is it gonna be just stop questioning and start listening then you'll really see

The enemy plans laid in your hands look in the mirror no excuse can be given excuse are lies just in disguise open up your eyes and real lies the ones that we tell ourselves because we refuse to ask YAHUAH for some help self centered his courts you can't enter you ain't got no praise just a bunch of complaints the what's the whys the who's who cares the alibis to try and conceal the lies

I feel some type of way I feel it every day I can't get ahead I remain in my head don't tell me that I'm wrong listen to my song pause to understand you say you got a plan

I feel some type way way way I feel some type of way way way I feel some type of way way way I feel some type of way I feel some type of way

Through the heart ache and pain I've learned how to maintain to keep from going insane in the membrane jumping around giving praise this ain't the house of pain looking forward to later days in the land of peace and rest living without any stress Barak by the best in his presence i feel safe and secure don't worry anymore under his wings he leads me beside the still waters when life is a bother

I give praise to ABBAYAHUAH my father holds me close in his arms reprimands me when I'm wrong REPENT his forgives so I don't do it no more listen to the words of this song and you won't be lead wrong there is more to life then worldly possessions or people that leave that causes your heart to bleed I have someone that intercede for me YAHUSHA is his name YAHUSHA prayed for me

I feel some type of way I feel it every day I can't get ahead I remain in my head don't tell me that I'm wrong listen to my song pause to understand you say that you got a plan

I feel some type way way way I feel some type of way way way I feel some type of way way way I feel some type of way I feel some type of way

I got a fistful of words ready to hurl to all who will hear within the earth you talk about past hurt sit and congregate congratulations you lost your worth mental inability to visualize with precision indecisive moments on the whim decisions face collisions living life with a faulty vision believe that YAHUSHA has risen call upon his name in these last and evil days don't feel a type of way or you lose your way

I feel some type of way i feel it every day I

can't get ahead I remain in my head don't tell me that I'm wrong listen to my song pause to understand you say that you got a plan

I feel some type way way way I feel some type of way way way I feel some type of way way way I feel some type of way I feel some type of way

Living Sacrifice

Present your life as a living sacrifice to walk in life be the light of the world in a darken place salt of the earth walk as YAHUSHA did not just in word but also in deed cause there's a need to see the righteous seed on the earth which is dismayed plagued the signs of living in these last days wicked ways abound some just men have turned from the way not able to endure ain't been rooted nothing deep within justify living a life of sin won't repent lost in the world has truly given in a living sacrifice to show the world without what it really means to never to give in present your life it's a service to YAHUAH otherwise in the end he'll be the one to come and subdue you

Live your life as a living sacrifice forsake your ways in these last days and evil days so the world can see the joy that the father brings as a living sacrifice

As a living sacrifice

Live your life

Blessed are the poor in spirit: for theirs is the Kingdom of YAHUAH. Blessed are they that mourn: for they shall be comforted. Blessed are the meek: for they shall inherit the earth. Blessed are they which do hunger and thirst after righteousness: for they shall be filled. Blessed are the merciful: for they shall obtain mercy. Blessed are the pure in heart: for they shall see YAH. Blessed are the peacemakers: for they shall be called the children of YAHUAH. Blessed are they which are persecuted for righteousness' sake: for theirs is the Kingdom of YAHUAH. Blessed are ye, when men shall revile you, and persecute you, and shall say all manner of evil against you falsely, for my sake. Rejoice, and be exceeding glad: for great is your reward in heaven: for so persecuted they the prophets which were before you.

Live your life as a living sacrifice forsake your ways in these last days and evil days so the world can see the joy that the father brings as a living sacrifice

As a living sacrifice

Live your life

www.ingramcontent.com/pod-product-compliance
Ingram Content Group UK Ltd.
Pitfield, Milton Keynes, MK11 3LW, UK
UKHW040002200726
13854UKWH00001B/4

9 781667 127163